Dedication

This book is dedicated to all of the front line and essential workers who sacrificed their time and lives for the greater good. Thank you for your selfless acts of kindness and dedication. This book is also dedicated to the memories of our loved ones lost due to COVID-19. You will never be forgotten. You should know that those you left behind are now breathing on your behalf. May your souls rest in peace. Rest in Paradise- William Jackson 12-17-20.

Chapter 1

The News

Breaking News… "A new virus has been reported in Wuhan." Not hearing the rest of the news as I cooked dinner in my kitchen. I remember thinking, where is Wuhan? Before learning that Wuhan was in China. I started to recollect in my mind, I think a co-worker from my job may have mentioned that his fiancé is from Wuhan or a town right outside of Wuhan. Whatever the case, this disease seemed miles away from Canton, Michigan. Like many Americans who were at home during the Holiday break, I was more concerned with celebrating

3

New Year's Eve and dreading the day when my Holiday break would end and I had to return to work. Life continued as normal. I had a new granddaughter who is the absolute center of my life. Baby Alora is my daughter's first baby and I tried to spend every waking moment with her. As time passed, my daughter was beginning to trust me more with the baby. Many Saturdays were spent babysitting my granddaughter. I never thought that within a few months my granddaughter, my daughter, and most of my family would be reduced to impersonal video visits and face time appearances. Many milestones that grandparents look forward to would be ripped away from me. I wouldn't see her first tooth, or hear her first words. I wouldn't see her holding on to furniture as she learned to explore walking, I wouldn't feel her soft little hands pulling at my glasses, and I wouldn't be able to make funny faces to make her laugh. A virus in Wuhan, China, that seemed light years away, would shatter the lives of family, friends, and change the way I lived forever. The sad part is the report and news I listened to on December 31, 2019, never eluded that this virus in Wuhan was coming for me and those that I love. There was no warning, there was no preparation, and there would be in some aspects no hope of escaping the wrath of this pandemic. It was coming for me in Canton, Michigan, and it would be staring me in my face by May 12th. By May

5

22nd this virus would have me fighting for my life

in ways that I never could imagine.

Chapter 2

Life Before

Most Americans have a life that is a rewinding cycle of get up, get dressed, go to work, and repeat. Some of us find ourselves adding much more to that cycle. I am definitely that person. I work at the University of Michigan, I teach karate to elementary school children in Southfield, Michigan twice a week. I am also a school board Vice President at a charter school in Ann Arbor, Michigan; and I also serve as the

7

Chapter Historian for my sorority. It all seems insane as I write these things down, but in my life at the time, each was very important to me and a way to fill up my time as most empty nesters do. My husband Phil is a Department of Michigan Corrections Officer and together we have eight adult children. They all each have their own lives and we find ourselves alone with our 9-year-old Rat Terrier/Chihuahua mix dog-Cecilia.

We are a blended family. Phil and I have spent a big part of our life raising children. When the children leave home and there is no longer violin recitals and sports events, that new found time is replaced with community involvement and volunteering. We gladly accept the responsibilities that comes along with a rigorous schedule. We have convinced ourselves that our lives would have less meaning if we were mere world travelers like most couples our age. Although, I must admit that I really want to start taking cruises. For a long time, I have had my sites set on a carnival or celebrity cruise. The topic of taking a cruise is a non-negotiable for Phil. He is simply not having it. I can hardly believe that the Desert Shield, Desert Storm Navy Vet is not interested in taking a cruise. It was a battle I did not see coming from a man who spent a good part of his life aboard the U.S.S. John F. Kennedy CV-67. Veterans give you the full title of their ship, whenever you ask where they serve. It is how we military brats and

9

wives can identify the true Veterans.

Nevertheless, we are happy with our simple middle-class life. We live in an apartment in Canton. It is rather small and we have dreams of owning a home one day. Phil is a divorcee and I am a widow; we take responsibility for our financial status. Among many of our goals, we are working to save money to purchase a house. Phil and I are more than just husband and wife, we are friends. Literally, he is my best friend. We sit around for hours when he is home from work, laughing, acting out our favorite parts of movies, and writing. We met in karate. Yes, I married my martial arts instructor. People always love the story about how we met and there are so many layers to that story. However, the short form of it

10

is- we once worked together. He was a security guard at the school I worked at and I was a school manager. He casually walked into my office one day and started talking to me, sharing his life story and it has been love and karate since then. We had an amazing wedding on October 29th in 2016. Our wedding was held on the epic Michigan State vs. University of Michigan basketball gameday. If you knew us you would know that Phil and I would not have had it any other way than to have people choose our wedding or the Big Game. You have to be a Michigander to understand the rivalry- and it is a big one. However, the love of our family and friends was very apparent as we had over 100 attendees at our wedding. I often reflect during

11

the quarantine how difficult our wedding would have been had it been held during this time. It places a pause in my heart as I sit here in my living room in June of 2020 that the memory of family and friends dancing and laughing in a reception hall may have been blurred by social distancing requirements, masks and several CDC guidelines that will become a way of life for a very long time.

Chapter 3

The Beginning of Change

When you see your environment changing it feels like smoke and mirrors, you really do not realize that things around you are changing until you see the end results. It is as if you wake up one day and what you thought were gradual changes are now prevalent and an everyday way of life. I began to notice hand washing signs at several public places and within my place of employment. We were all being instructed to wash our hands for 20 seconds. I previously worked in the health field many years ago as a medical assistant and I also worked with children for more than 20 years. The proper way to wash your hands is a way a life especially when you

14

work with children. Washing your hands is the difference between catching the flu and taking it home to your family.

I grew up during a time when you watched the evening news as a family, so for me old habits die hard. Every evening I watched the news. I wasn't particularly looking for information about the virus, but I could not help but hear on the world news that the number of people dying from the virus was rising and at a rapid rate in Wuhan, China. It still never was a concern to me that the virus would ever reach the United States. I did find the number of cases spreading in parts of the world to be alarming. I still did not know very much about the virus but had marginal concerns.

15

On January 19, the news caught my attention as it was announced that the first U.S case of the virus was in Washington state. As the weeks passed, I began to pay attention to the fact that certain items in my local grocery stores were becoming scarce such as toilet paper, paper towels, Lysol, and bleach. The news also reported that there was mass hoarding as people began to panic in response to the growing pandemic. There were only two of us in our home and we had enough resources. I was not interested in buying toilet paper or paper towel in bulk. I really did not see a need to get caught up in the mayhem of running out buying and spending money.

For some reason, I was convinced that since I had the flu shot, I would have some protection from

COVID-19. After-all, I survived H1N1 and had not had the flu in years. Of course, the science of this disease later proved that a flu shot has nothing to do with protecting you from COVID-19. The human mind will make up its own theories when in fear. Phil and I are avid about getting our flu shots each year. Because he is over 50, he also gets a pneumonia shot. Although, we could stand to lose a few pounds, for the most part, we are very active and in pretty good shape. I think my mind began to reason with itself that my body had developed some type of immunity to COVID because we were in good health, got our shots every year, ate right and worked out. Whether it is accurate or not, I was one of the Americans who believed that this

17

disease was spreading rapidly in other countries

because they did not have the health system that

we have in the U.S. I believed that the one case

in Washington would be handled and contained

and that all would be well. In the meantime, I

started to see additional changes at my job. I

remember attending a conference on campus

where there were digital messages instructing us

to avoid hugs, handshakes and to limit physical

contact and sneeze and cough in our elbow. I

really thought that these were proactive measures

to keep our community safe from common

viruses such as the flu or a cold. I could not

conceive that these were measures to prevent the

occurrence of COVID because I thought that this

was a virus that would be quickly contained and

never have an impact directly on me.

Chapter 4

The First Cases in Michigan

In years to come there will be a time when we will take a pause to ask the question: "Where was I when they announced the first case of the Corona-virus in my city?" March 10th was when two cases of the Corona-Virus appeared in Michigan; the breaking news headline came across my T.V. I had worked late that day so I was forced to catch the 11:00 p.m. news. I think that was the longest wait of my life. Where in Michigan could the virus be? I have no idea why I knew in my heart of hearts that the virus would appear in Oakland County. Oakland County is a large county in Michigan- It is not as large as Wayne County, but the population is very dense and diverse. Although I do not live in Oakland County, the school where I teach karate is located in Oakland County and has approximately 800 students or more. At 11:00 p.m., all of my fears became a reality. It was announced that there were two confirmed cases of the virus in Michigan and a confirmed case in Oakland County. My heart dropped; I was not only concerned for my health but deeply concerned for the health of my daughter who had my infant granddaughter at home. My daughter is a teacher at the school where I teach karate, which meant she was working in Oakland County where the virus was. I cannot describe the internal fear I had. I just sat in front of the television unable to move and in complete shock. I have always been the caretaker of the family. I have always been the one with the solutions and recommendations for my children's health. Make sure you do this, or make sure you take that. This was a game changer because for the first time, I did not have any answers. As a mother and a grandmother, I did not have any answers! I was afraid- I was scared to death. Less than two weeks later, the local news would update us regarding the number of Covid cases in Michigan. The cases went from 2 to 10 and the numbers began to rise rapidly. Now the disease was in Wayne County where I live.

Chapter 5

Preparation

As a mother and wife, I have a reputation for planning and preparing for everything. In my mind, I needed to prepare for war. This was a disease that had made its way from China to my county in a few mere months. I remember calling my daughter and having a conversation with her. I told her to quit her job at the school. Mothers do not have the luxury to stop being mothers. We also do not have the luxury of not trying to protect our children. We do not care how old they are, we do not care where they live and we do not care if they have their own children or not. Our instinct is to protect our young and it is an instinct that you cannot rationalize. I told my

24

adult daughter with an infant to support to quit her job. I was completely prepared to exhaust every bit of my savings to pay her rent or to care for her family until this was all over. I was scared to death and there was no rationalizing with me. I wanted my daughter to remove herself from any possibility of getting infected and to stay in the house. As fortune would have it, there were emergency orders that were implemented in Michigan requiring that we shelter in place. All universities and schools were closed and ordered to stay home by March 16th. While this provided some relief from my worry; my family was not out of the woods yet. Most of my family had positions or occupations that would allow them to shelter in place and work from home.

25

However, my husband is a Michigan Department of Corrections Officer and the prison does not close its doors. He was required to report to work and it was highly unlikely that there would ever be any opportunity for him to stay at home. I can tell you as the wife of a military veteran, asking him to quit his job was out of the question. Being a Corrections Officer was something that he was proud of. He had been with the department of Corrections for 5 years. Most of the work that he was able to obtain after the military was primarily in security. He worked at the casino for awhile and then worked as a Security Officer in schools. He worked really hard to obtain a job in law enforcement. Being over 48 at the time had a set of challenges when it came to getting hired in law enforcement. We were both excited when he was hired as a Corrections Officer. Neither one of us really focused on the risks associated with working in a prison, nor did we have concerns about a pandemic. For the most part prisons are closed environments, so when communicable diseases impact the prison it is most likely due to exposure from vendors, visitors, or officers coming in. I would often ask my husband, more often than not if and when the warden or prison officials were going to implement protocols to keep the officers and prisoners safe. I had some real concerns that he had not been given a mask to wear. As an outsider, it just did not seem that there were enough preliminary measures in place to prevent an outbreak of the virus within the

27

prison community. Be it as it may, I would learn

first hand the realization of my fears and

concerns; as this delay in response would have

life threatening implications for me and my

family.

Chapter 6

The First Death

You often do not realize how connected you are

to other people. This pandemic connected us in

ways that many of us did not realize. Working

from home and being quarantined in the house

presented a lot of time to engage in social media.

As a member of a sorority, and school board

28

member, I was a part of many groups on Facebook and had connections within my community and surrounding communities. These connections became a mirror into the impact that this virus was having on the county where I live and in my community. " I am praying for you" were the type of messages that began to flood my Facebook time line as people I knew had family members that were being hospitalized with the virus. Within weeks from the first "Stay Safe, Stay At Home Order" the messages quickly changed from "I am praying for you" to "Sorry for your Loss". People were dying! My friends were losing their family members, friends, relatives at an unbelievable rate. The numbers of identified cases went from 10 to hundreds in

29

what seemed to be overnight. Hundreds soon turned into thousands. Just as quickly as the posts and notifications were coming.......there it was, someone I knew and had seen a few months ago was dead. State Representative Isaac Robinson had just attended the centennial celebration for my sorority on January 18th and within a few months he had succumbed to COVID-19. I just could not believe it. In the meantime, the news was reporting mass casualties of this virus at an alarming rate. It was as if I was living in a dream that had turned into a nightmare. The devastation was not only realized in Michigan but in Washington State and New York and Louisiana. We were on the verge of surpassing Wuhan for the highest number of cases and deaths from this disease. I was mentally devastated. "This could not be happening in my country, in my state, in my city, to my friends."

Information was rapidly changing so often times my worry and focus would change. I was not as concerned anymore for the safety of my daughter as I was now for the safety of the elders in my family. The initial information regarding the virus indicated that older people and those with underlying health problems were at risk for contracting the virus and possibly dying from it. Most of the immediate elders in my family lived in Las Vegas. My grandmother had recently moved from Illinois to live with my mother and my father. My Great Aunt Ora moved to Las Vegas several years prior to my grandmother. I also had a sister, my son and my daughter-in-law who live in Las Vegas as well. I took comfort in the fact that my parents along with my grandmother were all in the same household and were together. However, I was on edge because my grandmother is diabetic and my father had been recently diagnosed with cancer. Although my Aunt Ora's health was a bit shaky, she had not been diagnosed with any major medical issues. My grandmother has always done things the way she wanted. For an 87-year-old woman who can still drive herself wherever she wants, has her memory in tact and is more active than some 30-year old, there is not much that you can really tell her. Nevada was not under the same orders that Michigan was as the virus surprisingly had not hit them as hard. As a result, often times, I would speak with my grandmother and she would say that she had been to Walmart or to the pharmacy to pick up her prescriptions. Cautiously, I would encourage my grandmother to avoid going out to Walmart, instead I would ask her to consider having her groceries and medications delivered. Her response to me was that she had lived through World Wars and that a virus was not strong enough to keep her locked up in the house. I would not dare argue with her but respectfully asked her to consider going out in the early morning to avoid large crowds. My grandmother's response was that she would

33

consider my request but do not expect her to stay at home. I thought talking to her about her daily visits to Walmart and the pharmacy was the least of my worry. Little did I know that there was a far worse concern that I needed to contend with. My third cousin in Illinois was celebrating his 50th anniversary and my 87-year-old grandmother decided that she was going. She purchased a ticket to travel by herself to Illinois in the middle of a pandemic. My mother and I were horrified and tried over and over to talk her out of going. However, there was no changing her mind. She was going to my cousin Vermel's 50th wedding anniversary and there was absolutely no stopping her. I have never felt so helpless in my life. Mentally I prepared myself for the worse. My diabetic grandmother was getting on a plane to travel during a pandemic by herself. I am pretty sure I held my breath the entire time she was gone. Not only was I worried about her travels to Illinois and back, I was worried about what she would bring back with her. After all, my father had cancer and was undergoing chemotherapy and my mother has health issues as well. My mother is a Veteran from the Army Nurses Corp and is still very active in Health Administration. She was very vigilant in taking care of my father and my grandmother. She sterilized the house, bought vitamins for them to take and did everything she could to keep them safe. My grandmother returned from her trip from Illinois. Several days had passed and my mother informed me that she noticed that my grandmother had a

persistent dry cough that did not seem to go

away. At the time, testing was not readily

available in Las Vegas. My mother informed me

that she would do her best to quarantine my

grandmother in the house and monitor her for

additional signs of the virus like a fever or

vomiting, etc. After about a week or so my

grandmother's cough was gone and she presented

no additional symptoms related to the virus. Our

family was extremely relieved that we had dodge

that bullet. Or so we thought….. Our celebration

that my grandmother had not contracted the virus

was overshadowed by the news that my cousin

Vermel in Illinois of whom had just celebrated

his 50th wedding anniversary was dead. The virus

had killed him within 3 days of being diagnosed.

Our family had not escaped the tragedy of

COVID-19 and there was a heavy price to be

paid for an early March social gathering.

Chapter 7

The New Normal

Learning to adapt to the changes and orders issued by our state was an adjustment. Most people were working from home. It was really strange to walk my dog and see so many cars still parked. Prior to the pandemic, there were always so many people out walking their dogs. My dog actually looked forward to running into his canine pals and seemed to be a bit perplexed that there was no one outside. Activities like going to the grocery store were stressful. I chose to go to the Kroger down the street from my house. This was primarily because they were one of the first stores in our area to implement social distancing protections such as plexi-glass at the registers and one-way direction isles for shoppers.

Grocery shopping consisted of masks, paying attention to where you were going and staying six feet away from other patrons. Then there was the task of washing your hands when you got home, sterilizing the groceries, putting them away and washing your hands again. An average trip to the store with all of the sterilization was 1-3 hours depending on how many groceries you purchased.

Working from home was not too much of a challenge for me. The University has really good plans in place for working from home and I was well prepared for that. I was not prepared for the social isolation and not being able to physically engage with my co-workers. It was also a challenge because I had conference calls in the day time when my third shift working husband was often sleeping. We had to make some adjustment but it seemed to work out well. I learned to become efficient with applications such as ZOOM and Google Meet. I even facilitated social events via ZOOM to connect with co workers. I quickly discovered that working from home is quite rigorous because the work can be continuous and absent human interactions.

My husband was gone a lot at the beginning of the pandemic. He was often hit with back-to-back overtime, which meant that I went days without any human interaction. I was determined to do

41

my part to reduce our risk of contracting the virus. Each day he came home, I would have him disrobe at the door, place his uniform in a bag and spray the bottom of his shoes with disinfectant spray. I would wash and dry his uniform then sterilize his lunch bag and thermos. Under the circumstances and with no vaccine, disinfecting really was our only protection from the virus. Later we would discover that although our efforts were admiral, the end results would still consist of both of us contracting the virus.

The loneliness at home was unbearable. I looked forward to the face time calls with my granddaughter. Over the past few months, I have seen her virtually grow up online. My daughter

Ashley was very good about sending me videos of her firsts. She sent me a video of her learning how to stand up for the first time and her first few steps. Overtime I think my granddaughter began to look forward to my calls, she would get excited if she heard my voice on the phone and start to cry until she could see me on the screen. Now that she is saying a few words, we spend the first part of our video calls with her repeating Hi and Hello. I do not mind, I am just glad that she still remembers me. Until the pandemic hit, I had been a consistent part of her life since she was born. I had several plans for us. This summer we were going to take swimming lessons. I learned that a local swimming school offered swimming lessons for infants. I thought this would be a great opportunity for my granddaughter and I was really looking forward to her learning how to swim.

A few months before the pandemic, Phil and I joined a church. It had taken us the entire three years of our marriage to find a church that we both felt comfortable attending. I went to Catholic school and attended a non-denominational church with my Aunt in my hometown of Indiana. Phil was Baptist. We were happy that we found a church to attend in Southfield, Michigan. Church service and social gatherings were prohibited over a period of time and it took our church some time to establish remote services. We went a few months without attending our home church but often found other church services online to support until our services became available remotely.

Overtime I came to terms that my life was transitioning into a new normal. The truth of the matter was I was going to be working from home for awhile, Phil was going to be working long hours and I would only be able to video chat with my friends and family. There had come a point where I had watched all the Netflix and Amazon Prime that I cared to see. Prior to the pandemic I was not and avid television watcher and by April I was over it. I decided to do something constructive with my time in the evening and started an online candle business that I named

after my granddaughter, Alora Rose Candles. I

was fortunate to be able to find a candle supplier

that would provide me with all of my materials at

home and I was also able to create a business

shipping account through FedEx. It was

rewarding to have a craft that I enjoyed and one

of which that I was very good at. Things at home

were looking promising and I had established a

routine.

I also found a way to connect with my karate

class and started to offer virtual classes twice a

week. It was great to reconnect with my students.

I really missed their smiles and hugs.

Chapter 8

A Cough at Night

The physical toll that the overtime had taken on my husband was apparent. I was extremely worried because he was only averaging 3-4 hours of sleep a night and he had an hour commute to work each way. All of the information and research I had done about the virus said that it was important to get a good night's sleep to boost your immune system. I could see the fatigue and wear and tear that the excessive overtime due to staffing issues at his job was doing to him both mentally and physically. By now, the prison had enacted some protocols to keep both the officers and prisoners safe. My husband had finally been issued cloth mask that were mandatory and now required to be worn during his shift. Across the nation there was a shortage of PPE so the likely hood of him getting his hands on a N95 masks was slim to none. At this point, I was just glad to see him with some type of protection. Besides, I did not want to communicate too many of my concerns to Phil. The stress he was already experiencing was enough. I worked to make his days off enjoyable and did my part to reduce as much of his stress as possible.

We both suffer from severe sinus and seasonal allergy issues, so when I began to hear him cough during his sleep, I did not worry too much. The facility took his temperature every night before his shift started, so I knew that there were not any other symptoms associated with his cough. I encouraged him to take his allergy medicine, I mean after all it was April in Michigan-and most likely allergy symptoms. The dry cough was on and off for a few weeks and did not occur every time he went to sleep. I did notice that he was extremely tired, but after all, he was working 16 hour shifts so I just assumed that his fatigue was due to his occupation.

Many of my days after work was spent researching symptoms, or gathering information about the virus. Things were changing so quickly that I wanted to make sure that I had the most recent information. I noticed that one day as Phil was preparing to take the dog out; he expressed discomfort in his lower back. I really did not think too much about it because of his years in martial arts, he had some slight back issues. I was certain that the overtime and excessive hours on his feet was also a contributor to his back pain. However, there was still this nagging notion in my mind and a reference to a case or information I had heard where a nurse indicated that one of her husband's symptoms after he was diagnosed with COVID was back pain. I still kept the information in the back of my mind. Besides, from what I heard and read fever was a much more common symptom experienced by COVID patients and Phil never exhibited a fever.

Although the intensity of Phil's cough never increased, the frequency of his coughing began to

51

raise additional concerns for me. I tried to recollect in my mind whether or not he coughed this way when he was having an episode with his allergies in the past. I just could not remember and it really bothered me. As the weeks went by there were weeks when there was a lot of coughing and weeks when there was no coughing at all. By the end of April, I noticed that there was occasional sneezing. Again, I continue to attribute his sneezing to allergies yet I watched for signs of respiratory discomfort. I often would ask him how his breathing was. His appetite seemed normal, Phil always has a really good appetite and typically a loss of appetite for him is a good indicator that there is an issue.

Phil did not talk about his job often. There is a lot that happens in a prison that he does not want to talk about. However, over dinner one day he mentioned that officers were beginning to get the virus at his job. I had friends who worked for corrections who reported that they had the virus but they were in other facilities and not the facility in which Phil worked. I guess as a wife you learn to read between the lines. You begin to understand the difference in voice inflexion; you can tell when something is of a concern. For the first time ever, my strong, confident, Martial Arts Veteran was fearful. He never had to say it directly to me because his eyes communicated everything.

The Love Chapter

A Love like Ours

I was really great at being single. I had 5 children from my first marriage and I had being a single mother down to a rocket science. My children lost their dad; he died when he was 40 years old. It was difficult for them and a challenge for me. Every part of my life was focused on them. At the time I worked in a school, I understood and was well aware of the evidence- based research surrounding the outcome of children in single parent homes and I knew that the statistics were not in our favor. Dating was never in the equation for me. I was not interested in introducing a man into my home. Nor did I have time for the emotional rollercoaster that dating can bring.

And then there was Phil......Co-workers at the school I worked at told me stories about the "karate man" who taught martial arts at the school. The word around town was that he was a lady's man and had garnered the attention of all types of women. I was not in the least bit interested in being involved in a relationship and definitely did not need the drama of dating someone everyone wanted. I would occasionally see him walking around school grounds and quite frankly my first impression of him was that he was extremely arrogant. Interestingly enough our first interaction was NOT love at first sight. I am pretty sure it was disdain. One day he came into my office and accused me of acquiring a delivery of his safety patrol equipment. I typically ordered recruitment and promotional material for the school so I often had boxes from the deliveries in my office. Needless to say our first encounter did not go well at all. Days, weeks and months would pass by before him and I would ever utter another word to each other…. and just like that…. One day while I am working, he just walks in to my office with a box of Cheezits, takes a seat in a chair and begins to tell me the story of his life. It really takes a lot to impress me, but his stories of his travels in the Navy were amazing stories. It was as if he was telling me a bed time story. I was mesmerized. He was intelligent, had seen the world and he had a Boston accent (which I found adorable). Even with the connection that we had made, I was still very cautious about our

56

relationship. I kept our relationship very casual and friendly. After all we were co-workers and relationships at work can always be problematic.

Fast forward…several years of dating later, we are holding a karate sleep over for our students. He was very elusive and told me that he would not be able to attend the sleepover. I was a little upset, although I had volunteers to assist me, we had planned this event together and he promised that he would assist me. All the kids were in the gym playing and in walks Phillip. I thought that was strange because he told me he had to work and would not be in attendance. He calls all of the children to attention… which is what happens when the master martial arts instructor enters a room. Phil was considered a master instructor because he had over 30 years of martial arts experience. All of the children immediately stop playing and came to attention. He had a folder in his hand and he announced that he wants to give me a special award and rank promotion for all of the years of service I had given to the karate program. I was shocked because I really did not expect any recognition. As I turned away to see the children's reaction, I turned back around and Phil was down on one knee. It was not a rank promotion at all; it was a wedding proposal... I was to become his wife. We were prepared to fight for our love, not only did we have to prepare for COVID but COVID had to prepare for a love like ours.

Chapter 9

Scared Children

When your children become adults, you accept the fact that they have their own lives. Our children are pretty good about checking on us from time to time. We are very proud of our children. They are each so unique. It is funny because we have (2) Ashleys. Phil has a daughter name Ashley and so do I. Ashley, Phil's daughter is a Master Sergeant in the Air Force. My Ashley is a third-grade school teacher. Of course, the baby of our three girls is Jasmine. Not only is she the baby among the girls but she is the youngest of all 8. Ibrahim is our States Attorney. He practices law in Florida and is also the comedian of the family. Phil Jr or Tamkeen, is in the National Guard and is our gentle giant. If you saw him your first inclination might be to be intimidated by his size, but he is a sweetheart and a gentle giant. Mikey is the youngest of the boys and is an Airman in the Airforce, Mikey as we affectionately call him, is quite the artist along with his brother David who is our middle child. Last but not least is our very own "Master Chef" Larry. Larry lives in Arizona and is a Su chef. It is funny because I can actually remember his first dish he cooked when he was 8… eggs and hotdogs.

As the pandemic progressed, we noticed that our children were checking in on us more often;

specially our youngest Jasmine. The media reports indicate older individuals were succumbing to the virus at an alarming rate. In Michigan the first few deaths from the pandemic were middle aged adults around Phil's age; He is 54. I am 7 years younger than Phil. However, there were reports of deaths of persons in their late 40's as well. Phil and I are certain that our children were armed with this knowledge and information as well. We could definitely hear the level of concern in their voices whenever they called. We both took great care not to mention our day-to-day concerns. The last thing we wanted to do was cause panic among our children. It was more important to us that they focus on their own health and the health of their children. Phil Jr. has two daughters: Aubrey and Autumn. Larry has two sons: Mikah and Karsyn. We did well with masking our concerns and keeping the focus on making sure they were taking care of themselves and being safe. Most of our children work from home with the exception of some of our military children. One is actually on deployment. We were fortunate that the virus had not impacted our children and their families.

Chapter 10

False Hope

May in Michigan is when spring really begins. It is a well-known fact that on any given day you can experience all fours seasons in the same day. Yes, it is true; winter in the morning, spring in the mid afternoon, summer in the late afternoon and fall at night. We dress in layers in this state and you do not want to get caught without an umbrella in your car. The beginning of May brought a sense of calm and hope for me. There was something in the air that made me feel we were getting closer to the end of this pandemic in our state. There were still hundreds of cases daily, but the number of deaths began to slowly decline as reported on our local news. There were more testing sites available to the general public and the ability to identify individuals who were infected was becoming more normal than not. Governor Whitmer was assuring Michiganders that we were approaching the peak of the virus and we would soon see a leveling in the number of cases. Although, she extended our state's Stay Home, Stay Safe Order, seeing a slight number in the decline of cases gave me some hope that soon this would all be over. I would day dream about the things that I would plan with my granddaughter during the month of May. My first plan would be to take her to the park in her stroller.

At home it appeared that Phil was getting better. His cough was subsiding and the sneezing was completely gone. He would still complain about back aches but we contributed his pain to his long working hours and the lengthy amount of time he spent on his feet at work. I was certain that the rather large combat boots he wore to work was also a contributing factor. Those boots weighed a ton and I could never imagine wearing something so heavy on my feet for 16 hours, but that was my big strong man, gearing up everyday to go to work.

I am an optimist by nature; Phil thinks it is so adorable that I actually wake up happy. Yep, I spring out of bed every morning. I have always been that way; I am just a very cheerful riser. It is funny because my youngest child is the complete opposite of me, she has to be the grumpiest person I know getting up in the morning. I think God has a sense of humor and made her that way to balance out our family. My optimism gave me hope that even with the extension of the Stay Home Orders that "this would soon be over." I think I said this to myself when I woke up every morning. Of course, like many Michiganders, I listened to the Governor's advice and took walks outside while still observing social distancing. On Phil's off days, we would visit Heritage Park in Canton. We have nicked name the park "Duck Park" The park is full of ducks on the pond who are very comfortable around people. Although it was stated that masks did not have to be worn when going outdoors, Phil and I still wore our mask. One of the things that bond us together is our genuine concern for other people. We often worried about Phil being a carrier of the virus because of his on-going exposure at the prison. We certainly did not want to be responsible for spreading the virus to those in the community. Despite recommendations of not needing a mask outdoors, we decided we would just take the extra precaution to keep those around us safe and wear our mask during our visits to the park.

Phil mentioned that many of his coworkers were getting tested. The state made it easy for essential and front-line workers to get tested. I would often encourage Phil to get tested, however he was very reluctant. He informed me that his job was

monitoring the officers and he would be sent
home if he had a fever or sent for testing if he
exhibited symptoms at work. I was a little
uncomfortable with that response because new
information was coming which indicated that
some people do not exhibit or present a fever but
still may be positive and carriers of the virus.
Nevertheless, I left well enough alone and did not
push the issue any further. Besides, all signs
regarding his health gave me a sense of hope that
all was well with him. We would later find that it
was indeed a false sense of hope.

Chapter 11

A Dog Nose

Now that all of the children are gone, our dog
Celia or CeeCee as we call her is our only child
and baby at home. We are pretty sure that she
knows this. She would have easily been a therapy
dog had it not been her selective approach to
making friends with humans and other dogs.
Either CeeCee likes you or she doesn't. If she
does not like you, she has no problem letting you
know. We think our little Rat Terrier/Chihuahua
really believes that she is a Rottweiler or German
Shepard, she is a small dog with a large dog
attitude, but we love her. She is very protective
and loyal.

Phil and CeeCee did not get along when they first met. Phil lost his dog Princess when he was a child and vowed to never get attached to another dog. However, CeeCee had different plans. A few years ago, Phil became ill with a pretty severe cold. To CeeCee, this was her opportunity to bond with Phil. She made it a point of jumping in the bed with him as he shivered from his fever and followed him around the house wherever he went while he was sick. They have been best pals ever since. When Phil is able to come home on time and is not scheduled to work overtime, he usually gets home in the early morning. CeeCee gets excited when she hears the door open because she knows that Phil is taking her for her daily morning walks.

73

I read somewhere that Teddy Roosevelt owned Rat Terriers. It is my understanding these dogs have a keen sense of smell. CeeCee seems to know when we are sick or ill even before we do. I cannot say for certain that she can sense illness, and I am not in the least bit implying that she can detect when someone has COVID. I can only attest to her peculiar actions prior to my COVID diagnoses.

A few days before I became ill from COVID-19 I noticed that CeeCee was behaving oddly. She is a very affectionate dog and loves to give hugs. However, she is a dog who likes her independence. She has a special chair in our living room that she sleeps in. Occasionally, she pounces in our bed but this is never for a long

74

time. For the most part she likes her space. She also does not have a habit of following me around- unless of course like most dogs she wants something or she wants to play. I noticed that for a few days CeeCee was following me everywhere I went. If I went to the bathroom she would wait outside of the door. If I sat in my chair to watch T.V. she would jump in my lap and would not move. A few days I found her sniffing me very oddly. I found this behavior very peculiar because I had never seen her behave this way. One day she was sniffing the middle of my chest so hard, she just planted her nose there and I had to pull her away. Cee Cee is getting up in age. She is now 9 years old and has some gray hair, but for an older dog she plays like a puppy. She can still jump and play and is very healthy. I was a bit concerned because sometimes dogs will behave oddly if they are not feeling well or in some cases if they are dying. Was my old gal getting senile from age? Did my dog know something about my health that I didn't?

Chapter 12

A Mother's Day to Remember

I am not a person that gets overly discombobulated when I do not get gifts for certain Holidays; Mother's Day is not one of those Holidays. I am an excellent mother and I expect to be celebrated, either with a card, or I'll take a phone call for that matter. This is never an issue because my children do a good job celebrating me for Mother's Day. Phil of course does an excellent job. On May 10, I woke up to a beautiful bouquet of mixed flowers and a card. As the day progressed, the text messages and calls from the children started pouring in. Phil and I were still quarantining ourselves from our

77

children so we did not expect to see any of them for any holidays coming up soon. So when I heard a knock at the door, I just assumed that it was a delivery. Most deliveries were accompanied by a few quick knocks and bye bye delivery guy. He or she was nowhere to be found. This knock was different, it was more than three knocks. My inner mother and connection to my children convinced me that it was one of them. I immediately grabbed my face mask and went to the door. As much as I love my children, I knew that we would have to talk through the door. I still had concerns that Phil may be a carrier from his exposure at the prison. I was not taking any chances with exposing them to the virus. I opened the door and it was my son-in-law

Matthew. Matthew is my daughter Ashley's husband. He is a sweetheart and really good to my daughter. He placed a bag of flowers with a Mother's Day card on the ground and stepped back. We talked for a while and I thanked him for the delivery. He told me he had to get back to my daughter and granddaughter. It was a pleasant surprise to see him.

Ashley and Matt had given me a bag of my favorite candy, cherry sours along with chocolate hershey kisses. I was in candy Heaven.

My Mother's Day was spent quietly at home. Phil and I ordered dinner from an Italian restaurant from down the street. We often went there to eat before the pandemic and we made sure to continue to support them. The food and

79

customer service is unmatched. My other children called throughout the day to inform me that some of my other gifts may be delayed. The virus was causing many deliveries to be delayed from Amazon and FedEx. Considering we were in the middle of a pandemic; I really didn't complain much about deliveries as they still managed to arrive in a reasonable time.

Phil is usually off from work on Sundays and Mondays so I try to stay up with him for a little while. This Sunday would be different. It did not matter what I did I was just very lethargic. I went to sleep before 9 p.m. which is extremely early for me. They say old habits die hard and I must say this is very true. I had bad habits from late nights of homework when I was in college. My early bed attempt would be a failure because my sleep would be abruptly interrupted in the middle of the night. I wish I could say what time of the night I woke up; but honestly, I do not remember. What I do remember is that I woke up feeling like someone had set my entire body on fire. I am a 47-year-old woman and I immediately thought that this must be one of those "hot flash" side effects of menopause many of my friends mentioned. I stumbled from our bedroom down our hallway past Phil and into the kitchen. I guess the expression on my face or my look of agony gave him cause for concern. He asked me if I were o.k. I told him I am not really sure but I feel like I am burning up from the inside. I drank a few bottles of water and went back to lie down. During the night I just remember tossing and turning. Phil said he came to check on me during the night because I was moaning and mumbling in my sleep.

Monday morning came and I still felt very hot. I took two extra strength Tylenol which seemed to bring me some short-lived comfort; before I knew it, within maybe an hour, my body was on fire again. This time the symptoms were accompanied by other symptoms and every muscle in my body ached. I called my mother to tell her how I was feeling. She told me I should continue to take the Tylenol and take my temperature often. She said to keep an eye on my symptoms. She seemed to be really concerned and mentioned to me that her research said to gargle with hot salt water. She said if I had the virus this may prevent it from spreading to my lungs. I had pneumonia twice when I was a little girl. Both occurrences happened before I turned 5 years old, so I already had compromised lungs. I am certain that this is what may have worried my mother. As a nurse, she knew that there may be serious implications for me if I caught a COVID pneumonia.

I continued to do home remedies throughout the day like drinking tea, taking vitamin C and eating fruit. I did not have much of an appetite but seemed to want pineapples all the time. Monday evening I recalled seeing a COVID testing sign

83

on the door of the CVS down the street from my apartment. I looked up COVID-19 testing near me and found that there was a rapid result testing site in Dearborn and I could have my results within 15 minutes of testing. I completed the on-line form which asked questions related to COVID-19. There were the standard questions: Have you traveled outside of the country? Have you had a cough, fever, vomiting or diarrhea? Once I answered the questions on the on-line form, I was able to make an appointment to get tested on Tuesday, May 12 at 12:45 p.m. I sent text messages to my sister Diyana in Montana and told her that I was going to get tested for the virus. My sister Diyana and I are really close and I knew that she would not rest until she knew my

84

results. She checked on me every hour until Tuesday arrived. Phil had to go to work Tuesday afternoon which meant I was going to the testing site by myself. I tried to be brave for everyone but in my mind I was scared to death. I took out my rosary that I had bought a few months before the pandemic and began to pray…"Jesus, please do not let me test positive."

Chapter 13

Testing Day

Testing day was here. I came to terms with the fact that I had to put on my big girl pants, take some Tylenol and haul it to the testing site. I made sure to leave the house early just in case I got lost and to also give myself additional travel time. I wasn't sure how I would feel driving because the fever caused sleeplessness and I was quite tired all the time. I pulled out around 11:15. This would be more than enough time considering Canton, Michigan on a good day is about 20 minutes away from Dearborn, Michigan.

The ride was decent. Since I love music, I listened to the radio all the way there, I found it soothing and calming and a way to block out any anxiety. I also enjoyed having the air conditioning in my car blow directly on my face. My fevers were pretty severe so the direct cold air was a relief. Even though I was in the car by myself, I drove with my mask on. I wanted to make sure that I wasn't touching my face as I traveled. I knew that the personnel at the testing site would likely have Personal Protection Equipment but I wanted to make sure that I did my part to be safe. As luck would have it there was construction on Southfield Freeway near my exit. The GPS was instructing me to exit onto Michigan Avenue East but this exit was

88

completely blocked. I kept thinking how glad I was that I left home early. The navigation system rerouted me and I was able to loop around and make it to Michigan Avenue East. As I approached the testing site, I saw two Dearborn Police Officers sitting in SUV's parked by what looked like the entrance to the testing site. I pulled up to one of the vehicles and asked the officer if this was the testing site. He said that I was in the right place and to just follow the signs. The first sign was a sign instructing me to be prepared to show proof of an appointment and to have my paperwork ready. My paperwork included my identification which in my case was my driver's license. I proceeded to the next sign which was about 20 feet a head of the last sign.

This sign instructed me to proceed with my windows rolled up and to only let my window down slightly when asked. There were orange cones that were made into driving lanes. The Army National Guard was present and giving directions and there were white tents set up. I proceeded to follow the signs and arrows. The testing personnel consisted of what appeared to be volunteers and nurses... They were all standing in a row about 10-15 feet apart. I noticed that the car in front of me had a different set of tasks to complete at each station. I arrived to the first station where I was handed a piece of paper from someone who was using one of those garbage pick-up sticks you see people use when they are picking up trash on the side of the highway. I read the paper while waiting to move up after the car ahead of me proceeded forward. The documentation was information on COVID - 19 and some instructions on procedures for completing the test. There was a diagram that told you how to remove the swab from the package and how to swab your nose. At a glance, it appeared that I would be swabbing my own nose. I thought this was great because I had seen how the testing was done on the news and it did not look pleasant at all! It looked as though they shove that swab up your nose until it touched your brain. The fact that I was actually going to swab my own nose gave me some relief and removed a bit of my anxiety.

When I arrived at the second station, the volunteer asked me a series of questions similar to the questionnaire I had completed on line when I scheduled my appointment. It was difficult to answer the question with a mask on and the window down 5 inches. Nevertheless, I managed to complete my verbal inquiry and was on to the next stop. This time, I was instructed to keep my window all the way up and to press my identification against the window. The volunteer took information from my I.D. and there was a 2nd volunteer who came around to the back of my vehicle to get my license plate number. Once they were done, I was instructed to proceed forward where I waited for about 5 minutes. Afterwards, I was allowed to advance my car inside the tent. Inside the tent there were nurses dressed in full protective gear (face masks, shields and protective gowns). There were cones placed behind my vehicle to prevent the car behind me from pulling up and to allow me to have privacy. The nurses handed me a package with two long cotton swabs inside of them. I was instructed to let my window down a quarter of the way. The nurses explained that I was to take the swab and place it up my nose and rotate it clockwise in a circular motion for 10 seconds then counter clockwise for 5 seconds. I would then proceed to take the 2nd cotton swab and repeat the same process in the other nostril. Once I completed this process, I was instructed to place the cotton side down inside the package and hand it back to the nurse after each nostril was completed. The nurses warned me that the process would make me feel like I had to sneeze and if I did so, remove the swab and turn my head away from the driver's side window and proceed with the process again once the sneeze was over. Once the testing was completed, I was told that it would take 15 minutes to receive the results and I would receive a phone call from a 401-area code. A gentleman removed the cones from in front of my car and instructed me to park in a specific parking space. I tried to calm myself down while waiting for the results. I listened to music, I checked Facebook and Instagram. Nothing I did would ease my mind. I just kept replaying the last few days over and over in my

94

mind. Realistically, I knew that there could not be anything else that was making me ill. I mean for the most part I had not been out of the house and was quarantined. I had not been exposed to anyone with the flu or any other illness except the Corona virus. It just did not seem possible to me that the test would be negative, but I was still hoping by some miracle that the test would not be positive. I sat silently and prayed for strength to endure whatever the outcome would be. There is a saying that minutes turn into hours when you are waiting for good or bad news. This was very true for me; it seemed like a life time in that car. I looked around and noticed that there were volunteers placing papers on the vehicles of those around me who were waiting for results. I could not tell what the results were based on their expression or reaction. Everyone seemed to be very solemn. I did notice that once they received the paper, they were able to leave. I found this confusing because I thought we were waiting for a phone call. Nevertheless, I continued to wait. As I looked down on my phone, I had a missed call from a 401 area code. My heart dropped because I did not hear the phone ring so I could not understand why there was a missed call. I tried to call the number back but was not able to get through. My phone has done this several times by sending unknown calls to voicemail; I was hoping that did not happen with this call but it did. Just as I started to panic, the phone rang again. It was a gentleman on the other end. He asked me to confirm my first and last name along with my date of birth. After I confirmed this information, he proceeds to tell me that unfortunately my test came back positive. For a brief moment in time, my heart stopped. I felt like I could not breathe in that moment. He further stated to remain in my car and that someone would be out to place my results and additional information on my windshield. Anything he said after that was a blur and I honestly cannot remember much of the conversation beyond the paperwork. What did this mean for me? Would I get really sick? Most importantly, would I die from this disease? It was not very long before a volunteer placed the paper work I was told I would receive on my window. After the volunteer left, I exited my car and retrieved the paperwork from my windshield. I sat back in my car and opened the paper. There it was, Positive. The word positive was highlighted in pink. There was additional information given regarding what the virus was and what signs to look for that may need further medical attention or hospitalization. The information also said to quarantine at home and that most cases of COVID-19 were mild. Before I pulled out of the parking lot I sent a text message to my sister and husband. I then proceeded to call my supervisor. I could barely say anything after the word positive. I began to cry. She was very reassuring and told me that having the virus was not a death sentence. She also advised me not to focus on the number of deaths reported daily by the media but instead to focus on the number of infected who had recovered from the virus. We both agreed that at the time it was unfortunate that this number was not reported as frequently as the number of people who survived the virus. She was very supportive and asked me if I needed any medication. She said the best recourse and treatment would be to go home and rest and try to take care of myself. I did not have the heart to call my mother because I knew as strong as she is; this news would be of some concern for her and I really did not want her to bare that worry. The drive home was long. I honestly do not know how I made it home given the state of mind that I was in at the time. When I finally arrived home, I rushed out of my car quickly. I was confirmed as having the virus and wanted to get inside of my house as quickly as possible. All I could do when I opened my door was sit on my couch and stare at a blank television screen. I did not want to hear any news about the virus. The next few hours would be painful as I had to call my family to let them know that I tested positive for the virus. Beyond my cousin who passed away, I was the first in our family to be diagnosed with the virus. The first call was made to my youngest daughter; I called her first because I did not want to risk her finding out from her other siblings. I needed to be able to console and comfort her as she was going to be very upset. With her biological father being deceased, the prospect of losing another parent would be devastating for her. I placed the call and she answered the phone. I started with small talk asking about her cat. She has a cat that I became very attached to; Gemini. She let me pet sit for her cat as she prepared to move in with her roommate. Gemini was a funny cat who I grew to love over the few short months that I had her. She told me Gemini was doing fine and that she was adjusting well being in a new place. I took a deep pause and told my daughter that I had tested positive for COVID. I could hear a brief silence on the phone and she began to cry. "What does that mean?" "Are you going to die?" she asked. I assured her that it appeared that majority of my symptoms were

101

mild and that I took really good care of myself before I got COVID so I should be fine. I told her that I needed her to be calm and strong because I would need her support and that she could not give it to me if she was upset. My heart was at the bottom of my chest. No mother wants to hear their children cry, it is just as painful as when they are infants and they cry. It does not matter how old they are, when a mother hears her children cry you simply feel helpless. This is particularly true when you do not have the answers and particularly cruel when you cannot hug or touch them to provide comfort. This virus would prove to be cruel in so many ways and on so many levels.

Chapter 14

The Worst Is Yet to Come

Each day with this virus felt like ten days all wrapped up in one. I had some regrets for educating myself so much about the virus. I knew more than I should, but didn't know enough. That seems to be the going scenario, not with just the information I had, but with the information that was being shared from the media. Most of my days were spent popping Tylenol like candy. I would feel like I was on fire, take two extra strength Tylenol, and then repeat the process two hours later. Misery is an understatement. Most of the days were a fog, as I was extremely lethargic and tired. It took most of the day for my body to recover. Ironically, I would feel a burst of energy everyday between 7 p.m. and 9 p.m. This is the time I would try to pack as many chores into those two hours as possible. My appetite was a complete joke; the only thing I could stomach was canned pineapples. At the onset of my illness, I would want chicken noodle soup, but over a period of time this proved to be an irritant and my meal of the day was sliced, or diced pineapples. Although, I was lethargic, there were times where I wanted to go to sleep but I was afraid to. I convinced myself that if I stayed woke as long as possible, I would not develop additional symptoms. I was so worried about the virus moving to my chest and developing into pneumonia. There was always the looming thought that if I developed pneumonia, I would

104

die as I could not rid my mind of the fact that I had pneumonia twice as a child.

I avoided sleeping in our bed and felt more comfortable on our reclining couch. Night sweats were the worst and each morning I was soaked and wet from sweating. However, I was still very positive that this would just be no worse than a really bad cold or a bout with the flu. I could do this; I kept telling myself I could do this. I mean between my husband and me, I was the one, who watched what I ate, who took my vitamins, limited the amount of alcohol beverages I had. Phil appeared to be fine. He was eating whatever he wanted to eat, exercising, and moving around just fine. I believed that if he was o.k. then I would definitely beat this virus. I was confident of it.

Approximately 9-10 days went by and my symptoms seem to cycle through a process, fever, a mild cough, sneezing and sleeping. This was my regular routine and I was o.k. with this. I was experiencing a slight heaviness in my chest but nothing that I felt I should be alarmed about. On May 20th, I woke up and called my mother. She worried about me if she did not get a daily check in. If you knew my mother, you would know that she would not be content with a simple phone call. She would want to talk to me. My mother could tell how severe things were getting for me simply by listening to me speak. This day I actually felt better. I was moving around a lot earlier than normal. I was actually doing house chores and it was before 10 a.m. In my mind I had beaten this virus and I felt really good about it. On the phone call with my mother that day, she commented that I sounded a little winded but I seemed to be in good spirits. I told her that this was a good day for me. She said that she was glad to hear that I was doing better and to contact her if I developed any additional symptoms or complications.

Our oldest daughter Ashley was home from Colorado. She is my bonus daughter and Phil's oldest child. We both had an Ashley, so now we have (2) Ashleys. She was going to bring us dinner and drop it off at our door. She called ahead to ask what we wanted for dinner but of course I did not have an appetite. I just wanted

Pedialyte and Gatorade. I stated earlier that this

virus is unpredictable and I was not joking.

As I was cleaning the house, I felt a wave of heat

come over me and I felt syncopic. I sat down for

a moment gasping to catch my breath. In my

mind I thought, I probably over did it with the

house cleaning. If I sat down for a minute, I was

certain to catch my breath. Breathing difficulties

were occurring from time to time. I waited for

about 15 minutes and with each breath, my chest

felt heavier and heavier. It felt as if I was

drowning from the inside out. I very slowly

walked to the bathroom because my eyes felt like

they were on fire. When I looked in the bathroom

mirror, I could see white thick tears streaming

108

from my eyes. I was horrified. "What was that?" Nothing I read or listened to mentioned white tears as a symptom. Somehow, I made my way from the bathroom and sat down. Unable to speak, I whispered to my husband that I was unable to breathe and that I would need to call 911. Phil was trying very hard to remain calm but his facial expression was one of sheer horror. I picked up my cell phone and called 911. I could no longer talk and could only whisper at this point. The 911 operator asked me a series of questions but at this time I felt like I was falling in and out of consciousness. Phil stared blankly as he looked at me, he seemed to be frozen. I did not want to make a bad situation worse and it seemed as though he may have gone into some type of shock. I managed to tell him to open the door because the operator said that the EMT's were fast approaching near my door. The emergency workers were dressed in full personal protection equipment. They were wearing hazmat suits similar to the ones I have seen on television or in movies where there is some type of airborne cotangent. Once the emergency workers reached my door, one of them stepped half way into the door and asked if I could walk. I really didn't feel like walking but I did not want the workers to come into my home and expose them to the virus. I mustered up the last bit of strength I had and walked outside without paying attention to the fact that I was not wearing any shoes. Immediately I was given oxygen to help me breathe. There were so many questions being asked and the EMT's were moving quickly to take my pulse, blood pressure, temperature- it seemed like they were doing it all at once. I live in an apartment complex; since the pandemic, I had not seen many of my neighbors outside. However, as I was being taken by ambulance, there were so many people outside. I saw one lady who seemed to be very upset and her companion was giving her comfort.

Much of what happened at the hospital has both strong and faint memories. It felt like I told the same story over and over again but with different people. Each time I repeated myself made matters worse. It was difficult to breathe, I cannot breathe is what I was saying inside of my

111

head. I just wanted to sleep and really did not feel like answering any additional questions. I was placed in a room in the emergency section of the hospital. I was so cold, shivering but was not allowed to have blankets. I remember asking if I could have a blanket but being told that I had a fever that went from 103 to 104 and that they are fighting to bring it down and could not provide me with a blanket. My head was spinning out of control. I had one of the worse headaches that I have ever had in my life. It felt like someone was rhythmically hitting me in the side of my head over and over again in perfect time intervals. I wanted the pain to stop and the nurses had given me Tylenol and other medication to relieve the pain but nothing seemed to work for me.

112

Although, I felt like crying, the pain from my head helped me to refrain from doing so; I really believed that crying would have only made my headache worse. Several lab technicians came in to draw my blood and I under went an additional Covid-19 test. I guess it was standard protocol to do so. I was in the room for what seemed like days. When you are sick as I was time really does not matter. Although I had not eaten, I felt like vomiting. I was very nauseous and unbelievably tired. After some time passed, I was given a series of additional tests which included an x-ray. They were able to bring the x-ray machine to my room so I did not have to be transported. I guess because I was so highly contagious that they did not want to move me throughout the hospital. A

113

few hours passed before the attending physician stopped by my room to inform me that I had pneumonia. I guess this fact explained why I was having difficulty breathing. There it was, the one diagnosis I feared was now my reality. I had pneumonia. Would I die from this? Could my already scarred lungs from childhood survive another round of pneumonia? Would I leave this hospital alive or was I going to die? These were all the thoughts that came flashing through my mind. I was not ready to die, I was not ready to leave my family, I was not ready to give up. I had been a fighter all of my life. Would this be the first knock out of my life or would I live to go another round with whatever the future had for me? At this point, I was not sure. For the first time in my life, I did not have an answer when I

needed an answer the most.

Chapter 15

The Fight Begins

Who can really say what happened at this point, I was ravished with fever, I had thoughts of dying and was fighting an internal battle for survival. By all accounts, I should not remember the details of what happened to me when I was hospitalized with COVID. I think that there was a part of me that felt and still feels it was important to hang on to these memories as long as I could. To forget them would be like forgetting apart of myself. That part of myself that was normal- the part of life that needed to be held on to- the part of life that included happy memories of my family and all of us laughing together.

116

An army of doctors and nurses were coming to take me to my room. I was going to the 5th floor. From what I could gather this floor had been deemed as the COVID unit of St. Mary's hospital. As my bed was being moved from the emergency room through the hospital, I could tell that we were taking a special route to arrive to the 5th floor. I knew we were approaching the 5th floor as I began to see brightly colored infectious disease signs placed on the door. Upon arriving to my room, I noticed that I had a private room. Understandably so. I was surprise to see that my room was private because the media showed overcrowded hospitals with patients in the hallway. Getting sick in May was the only advantage that I had as it related to this disease as

117

the number of cases were reducing and therefore the hospital was not as crowded.

Within the first few minutes, my attending nurse began to write names on a white board in my room of the number of people who would be taking care of me. I had a nurse, a tech and a doctor assigned to my room. All of them seem to ask the same questions: How do you think you contracted the disease? When was your first symptom? I was hooked up to a blood pressure monitor and oximeter to check my oxygen levels. From what I could tell my oxygen level was in the 80's. The nurse stated that someone would be in my room to take an x-ray of my lungs and that a series of test would be ran the first thing in the morning.

The nurses did everything they could to make me comfortable. I was initially given Tylenol for the pain and a series of medication to assist with reducing my fever. The medicine seemed to provide relief in intervals of 2-3 hours. I tried my best to sleep with each dose of medication but the fever and headache would wake me up. For me this was a clear indication that whatever medication I was given was subsiding. Under normal circumstances I would not have worried because being in the hospital when you are sick can render a sense of security that you have a chance for survival. However, COVID was different, by all accounts, I knew that there were instances when people appeared as though they were recovering from the virus but would relapse and sometimes die. There was not a moment that passed that I did not think that this would be my fate. Would I leave this hospital alive? That was the only question that replayed over and over in my mind.

I liked when the nurses came in my room, it was an indication that I was still alive. One particular nurse came in and looked at my chart. She said... "Your last name is Lawton- Did you teach karate class at PACE Academy?" I replied, "Yes." It so happened that I taught her son karate when he was a little boy- I remember him fondly. His name was Jaylen. Jaylen was a good student and always listened and took instruction well. His mother reminded me how much he enjoyed karate. She said that I was such an inspiration to him. I had Jaylen as a student when he was in 2nd grade. He was now in 10th grade. It was so good to know that someone I knew was taking care of me. The fact that I could remember things as far back as eight years ago was reassuring that I still had my mind intact.

Chapter 16

The Lessons

Karate was a big part of my life and that of my husband. One of the biggest joys I have is training and providing martial arts instruction to children. I received my black belt in 2012 from my husband, we were dating at the time, but that is a different story. Phil has been training in martial arts for more than 32 years. It was through assisting him with the paperwork for his program that I developed an interest in training myself. There were 10 adults who took advantage of Phil's offer to train with Phil. Him and I both worked at PACE Academy, (an Elementary School in Southfield, Michigan) at the time and he was offering adult classes. This was rather rare as he often did not invite adults to train with him. Phil is very much a traditionalist when it comes to martial arts training. His belief is that you are invited to train and such an invitation is an honor.

Phil had a lot of disclaimers about his martial arts training and relationships. He warned me that I may not want to continue to date him if he trained me. Could it be that bad, I thought? Well, much to my surprise he did not lie. It was very rigorous. Only 2 out of the 10 adults who began training actually made it to black belt. I was proud to be one of the few who made it. One of my first assignments as a newly promoted black belt was to begin teaching the younger students at

PACE. He actually trusted us enough to begin the program as a red belt. He had a lot of faith in myself and my dojo partner Rory.

Our first class had approximately 80 students and Jalen was one of the first students in our class. Classes were offered twice a week for an hour after school. PACE at the time was mostly populated with over 78% of students receiving free and reduce lunch. Many of them would not have been able to take karate classes, therefore, we were glad to be able to bring martial arts training to the school. It certainly is always great to hear that your program had a positive influence on a student 8 years later. Seeing that I was hospitalized, it was a relief to have some good news and be surrounded by someone who knew me. It also became apparent that I was not

only fighting for my life, but for the ability to

continue the legacy of doing what I loved and

that was training students.

Chapter 17

An Angel

Regular temperature checks my first day in the hospital had the same result- my fever was still above 101. The fevers were very persistent along with the headache that just would not go away. Other symptoms started to develop and my breathing seemed to be a bit more laborious. I wanted so badly to just be better. The unknown of what my next COVID symptoms would be concerned me the most. Each meal was forced down, as nothing really is appetizing with the loss of your sense of smell and taste. Nevertheless, I forced down as much food as I could tolerate; which wasn't very much at all. As expected, my x-ray was taken. They didn't move me from my room and actually took the x-ray in my room. A few hours later, the doctor came to see me only to confirm what I had expected; I had developed pneumonia in my lungs. During this entire ordeal, I think this was one of the few moments that I actually felt like giving up. I had pneumonia as a child and worried that the residual scarring on my lungs would only be compiled by my current case of COVID pneumonia. This was brought on by a sense of hopelessness and I just forced myself to go to sleep. I was so tired of fighting a battle that it just seemed like I was not going to win. My body was tired, my mind was tired and I was just TIRED. It was the longest time I had slept without a nurse or someone coming to check my vitals or give

129

me medication. As my eyes began to open and close, I looked up and saw that there was a very tall African-American woman in my room. She was dressed in all white and was not wearing a mask. She seemed to have a blunt like haircut. I remember her walking towards my bed and getting in my bed. Out of fear, I reached up and grabbed toward her hair because I thought she was going to hurt me. Her hair felt like wool or dry hay. It was very brittle like it had been frozen. She gently moved my hand away and without saying a word, laid down behind me and wrapped her arms around me. I remember that being the first time since I was in the hospital that I slept without being in pain. I cannot say who or what happened or if I was so medicated or if the fever caused some sort of delusion. What I can say that whatever that particular experience was or whether the lady in white was real or not did not concern me. What I do remember is that the experience brought me a sense of hope and peace. For a brief moment, in my mind, I was visited by an angel.

131

Chapter 18

Advanced Directives

My body was tired. Trying to breathe when your lungs are fighting against you is like trying to swim in water with 50lb weights strap to each leg. The nurses and doctors were trying their absolute best but I could tell by their eyes and the tone in their voices that I was becoming critical with each passing moment. One of the doctors came to visit me and asked if I would accept experimental treatment if they offered it to me. He described a series of medication- a cocktail so to speak that would involve medication to push the fluid off of my lungs and some experimental medication being used to treat COVID. He also asked me if I would be interested in receiving convalescent plasma from a donor who previously had COVID. I did not hesitate to say yes to all of these. The doctor prewarned me that the convalescent plasma treatment would take a few days because they had to find a donor that matched my blood type. I was O positive and had hoped that it wouldn't take long to find a donor for me.

Since it was difficult to talk, I often would text the status of my condition to one relative in the hopes that they would communicate my status to my entire family. I was so fatigue and did not have the energy to reach out to everyone. A few sentences written in a text message felt like a full-on dissertation due to my lack of energy. On occasion, I was able to glance at post on

Facebook. I saw where my children were asking for O positive donors who had previously contracted COVID to consider donating plasma to me or at least to the Red Cross. I was a proud mother at that moment to see how much support and resilience my children were showing. They were very brave and I was extremely proud in that moment.

In preparation for my plasma, I was scheduled a series of blood draws and other test needed to receive the plasma. It was explained to me that while I was waiting for a donor, I would need to sign papers and undergo testing. One of the forms that I was asked to sign was an advance directive. This document wasn't unfamiliar to me as it is standard procedure and I had signed one

134

before. However, for some reason, signing this advance directive really felt like I was approaching the end of my life. Feeling the way I did, there was very little room for optimism and I really was forced to face the fact that this could really be the end.

Chapter 19

The Nurse

Several nurses came in and out of my room during the course of my hospital stay. Each one of them took great care of me, but I will never forget Nurse Kiesha. Nurse Kiesha was an African-American fireball of a nurse who spoke very fast and was determined that she was not losing another COVID patient. She was very candid and honest with me. In fact her exact words were, "They are talking about placing you on a ventilator to help you breathe." "We are simply not going to have that." She brought a plastic tub full of devices, one was to measure my breathing. She told me to breathe in this device as hard as I could and to do so every 30 minutes to improve my lung function and lung capacity. Somehow her desire to not lose another COVID patient became infectious and was that spark that I needed to ignite a new desire to fight and persevere. I could feel her energy surge right through me. I was in the fight all over again. Raising my body was very difficult to do but I grabbed the side of the bed rail and used my upper body to push myself forward so that I could sit up to use this new device that I was convinced was going to save my life. Each breath was laborious but I needed to breathe as hard as I could in this machine and keep the indicator inside at a steady level. I tried my best but it did not seem like I was getting anywhere. I now know the device I was given was an incentive

137

spirometer. It certainly had the correct name because my incentive for going home was to improve my breathing and I was determined to do this.

Chapter 20

Childhood Pneumonia

I wish that most of the memories from my childhood didn't loom in tragedy, but this unfortunately was not always the case. As a child with pneumonia, I had several hospital visits. Back then, they put you inside of a plastic bubble to treat pneumonia. When you are a child, you do not realize how sick you are especially if you have good doctors and nurses taking care of you. Outside of being placed in the bubble, I really do not remember the symptoms of my pneumonia at all. I think being very sick and throwing up was the only memory I had before I was taken to the hospital. Children are brave, very brave- they don't seem to worry much about being sick or what could happen to them because of a disease. All they concern themselves with is playing, laughter, smiling and just living. There is so much to learned from children about life and living in the moment. You often wonder when the transition in life happens, when are they taught that they should concern themselves with tomorrow and fret over yesterday. That has to be something that is taught over a period of time because with all of the illness I experienced as a youth, I cannot remember any of the worrying or any of the concern. It was never a thought or concern to me that I would never leave the hospital from being sick with pneumonia. I never gave it a thought at all. I was just living for that day or days that I was hospitalized. I wish I had that bravery, that resilience, that fortitude- I miss

it now more than ever.

Chapter 21

Youth Never Dies

What were all of the things that I needed to accomplish in life that I had not yet fulfilled? I was not yet a homeowner. I wanted very much to own my own home. Apartment living was comfortable when you work all of the time. Phil and I spent more time at work than we did in our apartment so having a home didn't matter much to us prior to the pandemic. The ability to work from home was wonderful at first. I really didn't know what my apartment looked like during the day since I was never there. I did come to the conclusion that I needed to dust more often. Yes, dusting was not my strong suit and I could stand to get better at it. I mean in all fairness, I am just a little over 5 feet and everything that needs to be dusted is at least 6 feet... the refrigerator, the ceiling fan, the top of the cabinets- were all high so unless it was a window pane- dusting never was on my list of priorities. To establish my work space at home, I set up a cute little office space in my living room right next to our television. Although, most of the time I spent working from my dining room table. I guess the background had the best aesthetics for ZOOM calls- with the white wall behind me and all. This was until virtual backgrounds became a thing. Thank God for virtual backgrounds. I mean if ZOOM never invented another feature, they nailed it with virtual backgrounds. Virtual backgrounds allowed me to avoid the embarrassment of

143

background clutter showing up on my ZOOM calls. It was nice at first working from home, not worrying about traffic, what to wear, what to take to work for lunch, etc. After months of working at home, my apartment started to close in on me. I could not believe that my husband and I lived in a mouse maze. It was a real mice maze- which was approximately a little over 900 square feet. I am not complaining because we had a place to stay and were still employed. However, working from home for as long as I did help me put things back into perspective, I realized that I wanted a home to call my own. I had worked my entire life since I was 16 years old. I accepted things for what they were, I did not have to have the most expensive car, or fancy named brand clothes. My

144

first Michael Kors purse was bought for me by my husband, so I like to think that I was a pretty frugal and simple person. The fact that I was now in my 40's and had grandchildren- I longed desperately for a place that I could play with my grandchildren, and have friends over along with having a large kitchen for entertainment. I felt that I was in a place in my life where I had earned these things and worked for them- so a home was at the top of my list.

As I laid in that hospital, I reflected and focused on the fact that I wanted a house. I had accomplished most of what I wanted to accomplish in life, a great career, a good husband, great family, and all I needed to complete the circle was a home of my own.

Therefore, it became simple to me; I needed to live. There were so many things that I still needed to do in life and COVID was not going to rob me of those experiences. It could not and would not. As a 47-year-old woman, I needed to find the courage that I had as a 5-year-old and fight to live. I had made up in my mind that Denne Lawton was going home. Enough of this feeling sorry for myself, enough of this not being able to breathe, enough of this talk about convalescent plasma. I had also had enough of accepting that because I was an African-American woman with high blood pressure and a heart condition that I was not suppose to walk out of that hospital. My entire life was a statistic. I had been a single mother once, so statically, I was expected to live in poverty; that was a lie. My children did not have a father in the home so some of them, especially my boys were supposed to be in jail or dead; that was a lie! Now they are telling me that because I am African-American with COVID my chances of dying are increased; well, that was a lie. I am going home; it may not be today, it may not be tomorrow, but it will happen. I am going home.

148

Chapter 22

Speaking Life

People close to me know that for the most part I have a pretty positive outlook on life. I also believe that what you say you can do and what you say you can accomplish becomes tangible simply by speaking it. I believe that if I say that I will do something, then I must do it. That to me is how integrity works and that is how success begins; with the spoken word. Words define who we are, how we live and what we are made of. The words that you utter define the legacy that you create. I said that I was leaving St. Mary's hospital alive and that is exactly what I meant. I had spent more time than I cared to focusing on negatives and now it was time for me to speak life, talk about tomorrow, think about tomorrow

not as if it was promised but speak about it as if I

had a right to be there. I had a right to see

tomorrow, I had worked for it, and I wanted it. I

had a right to life.

Although I could not smell anything, a slight bit

of my sense of taste was returning. I began to

pick up a bit of an appetite. It is funny that the

way I knew my appetite was getting better was

by the choice of foods that I had selected for

breakfast and lunch while being in the hospital.

When I didn't have an appetite I picked food that

didn't belong together like applesauce and eggs

or orange juice and jello. I was back to putting

food groups together the way I liked them. Eggs

with bacon and toast, chicken breast with rice

and vegetables. My menu choices made a lot more sense than previously. This was the first indication that things were turning around for me. One of the attending physicians had come to see me and he immediately took a look at me and said "Oh my God, you look great!" I was glad to hear that, but I still paused for a moment to wonder what on earth had I been looking like before. I did notice that the dark circles around my eyes that made me look like a raccoon were fading. I am sure it was because I was now breathing better and my oxygen levels had improved. I no longer felt like my body was being set on fire. I actually started to feel like myself again. Walking was still difficult and I had a hard time going from my bed to the bathroom without being short of breath but the transition was better than it had been before. The doctor asked me the magic question… "Are you ready to go home?" My response was yes! I was ready to go home and I wanted out of the hospital. He told me that they would be running some more test on me and based on the results, he would consider sending me home in a day or so. This news was absolute music to my ears. I was so happy, but more so, I could see the doctor tear up a little bit. He said to me, "I am so happy to hear you say that you want to go home." "You were really sick and we were very concerned." This was the first time I had seen that particular doctor smile with his eyes. I cannot say if it was a miracle or not; I personally believe that it was. I had made a full recovery to the point that I was able to be considered for going home.

It seemed like days went by and there was so many blood draws and test ran before I was able to be cleared for discharge. Among my team of doctors, the one doctor I had to get past was my Pulmonologist. We needed his blessing before I would be able to see my husband again. It took a long time before the Pulmonary doctor came to see me, I heard him outside of my room talking to the nurse. Listening to his conversation it appeared that he was a bit reluctant to send me home just yet. I was very disappointed to hear that he wasn't for certain about my discharge but I was going to be understanding that whatever decision he made would be for my benefit. The moment of our conversation had arrived and it came down to whether I was ready to go home and what support would I have at home. I was very honest with him that after a few days, I would likely be home by myself because of the hours my husband worked, but I was confident that I could continue to recover at home. He then informed me that there were some slight traces of pneumonia in my lungs but that he would send me home and I could follow up by scheduling an appointment in his office. I was happy to hear this information, the nurses, doctors and technician had done all they could for me. At this point the rest was up to me and the effort I could put forth for my continued recovery.

Chapter 23

The Road Home

The day had come for me to be released from the hospital. It was great to be out of hospital clothes and in my own clothes. I had texted my husband that morning and instructed him on the process for picking me up. My transport arrived around noon to take me downstairs. I was given a list of prescriptions that would need to be filled, several inhalers, a blood thinner to prevent clotting and instructions to continue to take my vitamins to build up my immune system. The discharged nurse also informed me that any COVID test I may take after leaving the hospital would more than likely come back positive. I signed a release form before being discharged which indicated that I had been provided with managed care and stabilized enough to go home from COVID. I was not cured of the virus. It was important for me to understand that I was by all accounts still COVID positive. As the transport took me through the floor and to the elevator, the nurses played "Celebration" by Kool and the Gang. I thought that was a nice touch and definitely lifted my spirits. It was truly a celebration to be leaving the hospital and seeing my husband again. There was a part of me that wanted to cry but honestly, I still had some residual challenges breathing, so I saved the tears in order to save my strength.

I was glad to be home and back into my apartment, the first day I moved around slowly, but was able to resume most of my normal activities. I had lost a lot of weight. My clothes were practically falling off of me. Ironically, my hair, nails and skin were absolutely radiant. I have to contribute this to all of the vitamins that I had taken over the past weeks. Prior to going into the hospital, I was taking Vitamin C and Elderberry daily. The hospital continued to provide me with vitamins and Zinc every day as well. This was the greatest number of vitamins I had taken on a regular basis in a long time. I think the radiant vitamin afterglow was the only upside to COVID- if you can consider any upside to this disease. Days at home were up and down. I would often have severe fatigue in which I would sleep for 12-14 hours a day, wake up for a few hours and then go back to sleep. This would often last for a few days and then weeks would go by and I would be fine. The problem with COVID fatigue is that you just never knew when it would strike. When I resumed driving and began going to the store by myself, there were days when I could only drive a half a mile before the fatigue was so bad that I had to return home. Sometimes I could be walking outside or inside of the grocery store and become severely fatigued to the point that I felt faint. I tried to avoid going places by myself. The state of Michigan was still under some form of lock down, so there weren't very many places to go in the first place.

Since I was still working from home, I resumed work about a week after I was discharged from the hospital. I was glad to return to work, I think working made me feel as though I was getting back to normal. At times, even work became challenging as trying to remember things became difficult due to memory fog. I found myself writing things down quite often in order to stay on track. I would often forget a complete thought mid-sentence. It was apparent that I was suffering some form of memory loss since I had returned home. Was this due to a lack of oxygen? Or could it be another side effect from having COVID. The side effects or lasting illnesses resulting from COVID were still being identified. It was almost like a waiting game or in some

160

cases you may actually be the first person to present a new side effect from the disease. Whatever the case, my body did not feel the same and my mind did not feel the same. There were parts of me that were lost due to COVID and honestly, I was not sure if I would ever be the same.

Chapter 24

When Mothers Stopped Breathing

While I was in the hospital, I didn't really have a lot of time for social media. In fact, I am not sure if I even had WIFI access during my hospital stay. It appears that a flood of posts started to come in on my timeline and in my newsfeed all at once when I arrived home. A lot happened since I was hospitalized and returned home. I was a little reluctant to scroll through my post but did find my way to my page. There were so many of my friends and friends of my friends who sent their well wishes to me while I was sick. It made me feel good to see the outpouring of concern. I didn't feel like I was going through COVID alone. I felt a human connection through social media. I needed to feel connected because when I was in the hospital, I felt so isolated and alone. I was glad to see that I didn't see many "I am sorry for your loss" posts. There had been no deaths among my friends and family and those who I was connected with on Facebook in weeks. This was great news. For a brief moment it gave me hope that maybe the pandemic would be over soon. Maybe the deaths would stop, maybe the sorrow would stop, maybe I wouldn't have to see anymore "rest in peace" or "rest in Heaven posts". Was it over?

As I kept scrolling, I came across a post by a martial artist who is a mutual friend of me and my husband. It was of an officer with his knee on the neck of a man. The caption read "black man killed on camera by officer." I couldn't watch the post. There was a part of me that was hoping that this was a hoax because how could something like this happened in the middle of a pandemic? I immediately closed the Facebook app. I did not want to read or hear anything about this any further. About two hours later, I turned on the news to discover that it was true. There was a disclaimer before the video was aired which stated... "the image you are about to see is graphic." There it was…. It was a police officer with his knee on the neck of an unarmed black man. As I watched this video, I was still hopeful that this was going to end with the officer standing up and this being some sort of officer misconduct case. However, it wasn't. The officer

164

kept his knee on the neck of this man until he died and I just watched this on T.V. and it is real! I later learned that the name of the man was George Floyd. I was in disbelief. What happened? We are Americans and we are in the middle of one of the worst pandemics to hit our nation. What happened to the America that puts our differences aside and come together through a crisis like we did during 9-11? There is no time for racial injustice, to me there was no room for racial injustice or anything like this. We were all supposed to be standing together to fight a common enemy and that enemy was COVID-19. Is this the world that I fought so hard to be apart of again? Is this the world that I wanted so much to get back to? Is our country so divided that we

actually have the time to overlook a threat that
will continue to claim lives regardless of age,
race, gender or sexual orientation? Did COVID
not teach us that we are all human and that
anyone can die from this disease? Did I just
witness a grown man cry out for his mother as he
took his last breath? What happened while I was
in the hospital? … I was in shear disbelief. The
whole ordeal sent me into a deep dark depression
that I hadn't felt in a long time. There was a
cloud of confusion, fear, concern and dismay that
I could not simply shake off. I was grieving
because I felt hopeless. If we weren't willing to
put our differences aside and work together, what
would happen to us? I had to face the reality that
America still had a disease that we had not yet

come up with a vaccination for, and that was

RACISM.

Chapter 25

The Journey

Breathing some days was very difficult to do. For no apparent reason at all I would find it extremely difficult to catch a breath. The ability to video call with my doctor offered me a way to connect with him without going into the office. He continued to reassure me that many of my symptoms would subside over time. He was very transparent and honest that there was no conclusive information about side effects and how long I would have them. I tried my best to resume a normal life. By the summer time, Michigan lifted some restrictions on outdoor gatherings for youth sports. This was very exciting news for our karate program and my husband and I were ready to get back to training our students. We held an outdoor program and followed CDC and the local health department guidelines. We provided temperature checks, required all students to wear masks and required parents to complete a questionnaire. We also limited our attendance within the program to no more than 15 students. Although at the time, the mandate in Michigan allowed for more students to participate as long as the program was outdoors. It was so good to see the children and have the ability to provide them with an activity. We were really glad to be able to do this. I actually taught the classes with the help of Phil and two of our assistant instructors. We had do modify our instructions to maintain social

169

distancing. We did not do pad drills or allow the children to work with each other to avoid any physical contact. We were fortunate that we were able to host the program for about 4 weeks. Unfortunately, the number of COVID cases began to rise again and additional restrictions were put in place. Phil and I ended the program a month before the school shut down on October 30th and went completely on-line. Although we missed the children, their safety was more important to us.

Chapter 26

An Unexpected Side Effect

Phil and I found ourselves celebrating life and enjoying as much of the outdoors that we could during the summer. We were so glad to be out of our apartment and even more glad that restrictions did not prevent of us engaging in outdoor activity. We had talked about buying bicycles for some time and thought with the limited activities that were available to us, now was a good time. I think several people had the same idea because it was very difficult to find bikes anywhere. We had to travel 20 miles from our home to the east side of the state to find bikes. The bikes were a bit more expensive than we wanted but it was well worth the purchase to have an additional activity. It took some time to select our bikes. While we were waiting to make our purchase, I felt like there was something crawling on my shoulder. It was very hot that day so I was wearing a sleeveless top and shorts. I went to scratch my shoulder and I noticed that it was a strand of hair that was causing my irritation. I didn't pay very much attention to it; I mean it was not unusual for my hair to shed in the summer. Besides, I have very thick and long hair so a few strains here or there was no big deal. As we were leaving the bike shop and preparing to get into my husband's Jeep, I noticed that the back of the seat was covered in my hair. I was slightly alarmed but still just assumed that it was a collection of hair from previous trips in the Jeep.

As the days went by, I noticed that when I would get out of the shower each morning there were several strands of my hair on the bathroom floor. I still didn't worry too much and continued with my hygiene regiment. Until one particular day I brushed my hair and half of my hair was in my brush. It was at this point that I became alarmed. I immediately pulled out my phone and googled hair loss after COVID. I am not sure how I knew to attribute my hair loss to COVID, but I instinctively did. There it was, a famous actor had posted a video that her hair was falling out after COVID. I frantically began to look up other stories. There was a woman who showed a before

174

and after picture of her hair and she was completely bald in the middle. I was devastated. Most of the stories I had read stated that women who were COVID survivors had started to see moderate to severe hair loss. The articles gave various reasons but the most common cause among COVID survivors was that their hair loss was caused by a condition known as Telogen effluvium. Telogen effluvium is a form of hair loss that happens after a traumatic experience. It certainly doesn't get any more traumatic than having COVID and being hospitalized. I was yet again at a place with this disease where I was hit with an unexpected surprise. COVID kept true to it pattern of deceitfulness. Afterall, the disease can kill a patient who appears to be recovering. I should expect that this disease would allow my hair to flourish upon discharge from the hospital only to render me bald 3-4 months later from the trauma that I survived. Yet again, COVID showed no mercy and was coming after what was left of my mental health. A woman's hair is her glory. Of course, I would accept being alive and bald without a problem. My issue was the unexpectedness of this side effect and the inability to mentally prepare for it. It wasn't the hair loss alone that frightened me, it was the other unknowns about this virus that could surface at any given moment. I had heard and read of people who had survived COVID only to drop dead from a heart attack several months later. This disease was cruel and relentless. If I would later learn how that COVID had more indirect ways of changing your life as well.

Chapter 27

A Soldier's Death

As the media projected the possibility that a vaccination was in the near future, a bit of home loomed for me. I had a habit of visiting my parents and relative in Vegas every year. However, because of their vulnerabilities as older adults and the travel restriction and recommendation due to the new surge of cases, it just did not seem that I would make it to Vegas this year. My father was having several medical issues during this pandemic. He was fortunate enough to escape COVID but his past health issues had caught up to him. He was a Veteran and had served in every war since Vietnam. He was a retired Master Sargent in the United States Army. William Jackson loved the United States of America and even after his retirement he took a job with the Department of Defense and did a tour in Iraq. Both my mother and father are retired military. My mother retired as a Captain in the Army Nurses Corp.

COVID was the worse time to be hospitalized for so many reasons. There were limited resources available due to the number of COVID patients in the hospital. Nurses and doctors were stretched thin. However, in the beginning, my father seemed fortunate enough to escape all of this. He

178

was lucky to receive his care at the hospital at Nellis Airforce Base in Nevada. He was having a very difficult time with his health but each time he was hospitalized at the base, they were able to provide him with the care that he needed and he was right back at home with my mother.

My mother and father have one of the happiest marriages I have ever seen. Although William is not my biological father, you would never have known that by the way he treated all of us and how good he was to my children. When my children were growing up, they had wonderful summers with grandma and grandpa. They would take them to the beaches in Florida and all over the country. Sometime summers would be spent in their home in Smithville, Georgia. My youngest daughter enjoyed getting coffee drinks with Paw Paw (as she affectionately calls him) every morning at the local Circle K in Smithville, GA. At the time, I was a struggling single mother and could not afford to take my children on vacation or spend summers with them the way I wanted to. As a single mom I worked all summer long and never took vacations during that time. It was nice to know that I had supportive parents who could provide my children with those wonderful summer experiences.

One of the most heart wrenching side effects of COVID is the restrictions prohibiting family from being with their loved one in the hospital. I had read and heard of numerous stories of loved ones who died alone; or even more cruel, not being able to say goodbye or hold the hand of someone you love as they take their last breath. For a very brief moment during the pandemic, some hospitals relaxed this restriction as the cases of COVID were declining. However, in late November there was another surge in cases and hospitals were overwhelmed again with COVID patients. The nation was seeing an astronomical number of deaths per day. It is believed that this surge may be a result of Thanksgiving Day and holiday travel. It wasn't uncommon to see a spike in cases from COVID after a holiday. This was true for both Memorial Day, the 4th of July and Labor Day. Even though there was a surge after these holidays, America always seemed to bounce back and restabilize again. This was not the case after Thanksgiving. Things went from bad to worse very quickly. My friends were losing loved ones and friends at a rapid rate and Facebook was yet again flooded with "I am sorry for your loss" posts. I really thought that I was done seeing these types of post, but I wasn't. I attended four virtual funerals between mid-November and the first week of December. It was like the outbreak that occurred in March was repeating itself all over again.

I had become accustom to seeing a text message from my mom informing me that my dad was in the hospital. He was very ill, an exposure to agent orange during the Vietnam war and other health issues had taken its toll on his kidneys and he was struggling. On December 15th I received a

182

text message from my mother that my father was back in the hospital. This time was different. He wasn't in the hospital on the military base where the doctors were familiar with his treatment plan. Due to COVID he was in a different hospital where they were unfamiliar with his care. I was really worried because he was 71 years-old and in the hospital, alone. Although the hospital allowed my mother to be with him in the emergency room, once he was admitted to ICU, she was unable to see him. My mother who is a nurse was very familiar with the care that he needed. However, due to COVID she was unable to render the support that so many people need when they are critically ill. On December 17th, my father had three heart attacks. A man who served his country for 26 years and sacrificed

everything to make it back home from every war

he was ever in, died alone without being

surrounded by his family. Although COVID was

not the reason my father died directly. COVID

was responsible for robbing my mother of the

opportunity to say goodbye to the hero and the

heartbeat of our family. COVID had broken our

hearts and like so many people across the

country, we were unable to escape the wrath of

sorrow that this pandemic inflicted on so many.

On December 17, 2020, I joined the list of people

whose Facebook time lines were flooded with

that same song of sorrow; "I am sorry for your

loss."

Made in the USA
Middletown, DE
08 August 2021

45524767R00106